50 Fabulous Classical Monologues for Women

Newly Adapted by

Freyda Thomas and Jan Silverman

SAMUEL FRENCH

FOUNDED 1830

NEW YORK HOLLYWOOD LONDON TORONTO

SAMUELFRENCH.COM

IMPORTANT BILLING AND CREDIT REQUIREMENTS

FREYDA THOMAS

Freyda Thomas has a B.A. and an M.A. in French from Penn State, and an M.F.A. in writing from California Institute of the Arts. One of America's most well-known and oft-produced adapters of the classics, she has seen her work displayed on and off-Broadway, and at some of the most well-known regional theatres in the country, including the Alabama Shakespeare Festival, Northlight Theatre and A.C.T. in San Francisco, which recently produced her 5th adaptation, *The Gamester.* It was a finalist for the Susan Smith Blackburn Women's International Playwriting Award in 2000, had its world premiere at Chicago's Northlight Theatre and was produced by the Repertory Theatre of St. Louis in 2003. It is published by Dramatists Play Service, Inc.

The Learned Ladies, Molière's sendup on Women's Lib, was her first adaptation. It had its world premiere off-Broadway in 1991, starring Jean Stapleton, followed by an A.C.T. production in 1993 and a production at Florida Studio Theatre in 1994. In 1996 her translation/adaptation of Molière's *Tartuffe* (*Tartuffe: Born Again*), featuring the infamous religious hypocrite as a televangelist, had its world premiere on Broadway, starring John Glover. Both Molière plays are published by Samuel French, Inc. She is also the co-author of *The Mistress of the Inn,* an adaptation of Goldoni's *Mirandolina,* which had its world premiere at Virginia Museum Theatre in 1984. Her new Molière adaptation, *School for Trophy Wives,* a Hollywood romp, and *Splitting Heirs,* a farce inspired by Regnard's *Le Legataire Universel,* are available for production consideration. Several monologues from her works, and works-in-progress, are included in this book.

JAN SILVERMAN

Jan Silverman has a B.A. in English from Muhlenberg College, an M.A. in Theater from the University of Pittsburgh and an M.F.A. in directing from Temple University. She taught acting, directing and classical text analysis for 27 years at her last alma mater, where she also headed the graduate directing program. She also served the College Board as a member of the Advisory Committee on the Arts from 1978 - 1983. Many well-known actors honed their talents under her guidance, including Tom Sizemore and Marylouise Burke. She is the author of *Just So!*, a dramatization of Rudyard Kipling's *Just So Stories*, published by NPC Publications.

In her long and varied career, she has directed over 70 productions, including several of her favorite Shakespeare plays (*As You Like It, A Midsummer Night's Dream, The Merchant of Venice* and *Macbeth*), and a number of new plays in New York (Ensemble Studio Theater, The Village Gate, and Alice's Fourth Floor) and in Philadelphia (Philadelphia Festival Theater for New Plays and the Philadelphia Theater Company.) Two productions which she directed at Temple are her particular favorites: one was *Tartuffe: Born Again*, by Freyda Thomas. The other was *The House of Blue Leaves*, in which, long ago, Ms. Thomas played Bunny Flingus.

TABLE OF CONTENTS

Guide to Performing a Classical Monologue

YOUNG WOMEN'S DRAMATIC MONOLOGUES

A GUIDE TO PERFORMING A CLASSICAL MONOLOGUE

Actors performing the classics face a challenge, but more important, they receive a great gift—the words themselves. In classical text, the words are the full expression of the innermost thoughts and feelings of the characters, so do not be afraid of them! Rather than regarding rhythm, rhyme and "poetic" images as stumbling blocks, recognize them for what they are: windows that open directly into your character's heart and mind.

When Romeo says, "What light through yonder window breaks/ It is the east, and Juliet is the sun," he is not just talking pretty! He is giving the audience his inner experience—love is a vision of light to him. When Juliet, later, confesses her love for him, saying "My bounty is as boundless as the sea," she feels those powerful tides and leaping waves in her very core, in a physical, immediate way.

A metaphor has its roots in the character's inner life and experience. In *The Miser*, the title character, Argan, reacts to the theft of his strong-box, thus: "Assassin! Murderer! I've been assassinated...My throat's been cut. My money is gone...That's it, I'm a dead man...Oh, my poor, poor money, my helpmeet, my companion, my friend!" In *Medea*, Jason, a great sea-going warrior, tells his rebellious wife "As for myself, I am relieved to be/Rid of the tempest you've brought down on me/I've grabbed the tiller." The images that characters use are constructed of the stuff that makes up the landscape of their minds. To get a look at that landscape, take the image in the text and trace it back to its source. This makes for useful character analysis.

The verse form of classical text in English is iambic pentameter—that is, each line is composed of 10 syllables, with alternating stresses on each even-numbered syllable. Iambic pentameter was first used by Christopher Marlowe and then fully developed by Shakespeare; it is the rhythm that best suits the natural cadences of spoken English. As the speaker, you need to be aware of the rhythm but not driven by it. What drives the line, always, is its meaning, its action, its intention to affect and change the character hearing it, or in the case of these monologues, which you will be using as audition pieces or classwork, the audience. Regard the rhythm as the drum-beat in a musical line, or better yet, the heart-beat of the character. It's illuminating and also a lot of fun to search out irregularities in the rhythm of a line—they are clues to finding moments of disturbance and excitement in the speaker.

Rhyming lines, especially rhymed couplets, often frighten actors because of their overt artificiality (the lines, not the actors!). Actors want to sound "real," and dread the sing-song quality that rhyme can produce. But rhyme instantly appeals to the ears of the audience—rhymes are there to be heard, not hidden, and a wise actor will not dodge them but relish them. Again, the rhymes do not drive the speech—meaning and action still prevail—and in most cases, the rhyme will take care of itself if treated with a modicum of respect. Speaking in rhymed couplets is not as far removed from the new millennium as you think. Listen to rap for a taste of modern rhymed couplets!

Awareness of punctuation is key in understanding how to handle verse, and especially rhyme. Lines you are speaking should be stopped only by periods, exclamation points, colons or question marks. A comma, or lack of final punctuation, requires the speaker to drive through to the next line, until the thought itself ends. Remember, the length of the line and the length of the thought are often not the same, and you must go with the thought. Especially in the case of the verse monologues in this book, which are much more conversational than the norm, you must speak to the punctuation. With the following exception:

American actors in particular must guard against a tendency to drop inflection and vocal energy at the ends of lines—nothing will kill the sparkle of the language, and indeed, obscure its meaning, faster than that. Even a line that has no period at the end of it needs a sustained inflection at the end. A sustained or rising inflection is an invitation to the audience's ears that says, "Listen—there's more to come!" A British actor will tend say: "Friends, Romans, countrymen, lend me your *ears!*" because of the speech patterns in England, whereas an American will tend to say, ""Friends, Romans, countrymen, lend me your *ears*," because Americans tend to drop the energy of the line as they come to the end of it. A little bit of practice with a tape recorder or a friend or teacher, will help you overcome that habit.

Some rhymes are more important than others within the text, and you need to become aware of the varying functions of rhyme. Often, the writer is using the rhyme to make an important point stand out, clinch an argument or set up a laugh. In these cases, you need to give extra clarity and a vocal lift to the end of the first line in the couplet so that the moment is brought home at the end of the second line. Naturally, there is no need to hit the audience over the head, here. You just want to be generous to their ears and give them a little help—"let your discretion by your tutor." Consider the following examples:

From *The Learned Ladies*:

> And I for one applaud the time she chose a
> Moment to forget Kant and Spinoza.

From *Tartuffe: Born Again*:

> Right now, I said, I'll show you all the poss'ble
> Ways of beating Satan with the gospel!

From *School for Trophy Wives*:

> [Eve:] Oh, Chris, you know my lawyer says no.
> [Chris:] Where did you leave her?
> [Eve:] On a farm near Fresno.

In the first example, the "a" at the end needs to be upheld just slightly, with a clear connection to "chose." If you allow it to spill over to the next line, becoming a part of "Moment," you will squander the fun for the audience. In the second example, sustain the inflection on "poss'ble," so that it doesn't get lost in the phrase "poss'ble Ways," of which it is clearly a part. The adjustment is subtle, but the difference it makes is enormous. In the third example, the word "says" must be stronger than the "no" that follows it in order to deliver the laugh on "Fresno." In each case, your delivery will make all the difference between a crisp, funny moment and one that doesn't quite happen.

Classical language often presents such a rich banquet of words that the audience's ears can be overwhelmed. To make it easy for them to grasp the content of the speech, locate the operative, or key, words and find ways to stress (but not distress!) them. Operative words are literally those that operate, that run, the line. They are usually nouns and verbs, though not always. A good test is to imagine that you have to send a telegram, with every word costing 10 dollars: with your limited budget, you must keep the words you include to a bare minimum. Which words would you choose? Those are your operatives.

Beginning actors sometimes tend to treat all operatives within a line the same, hammering them out. Please don't! Think of each operative word's meaning, its sound, its texture, its length, its feel. Your ways of making them distinct should be as varied as the words themselves.

The language of any play is a primary element of its world. Iambic pentameter gives a certain size and emotional resonance to the play's events. Rhyme lends a playful quality and often seems best suited to comedy although Racine used rhymes in his very successful 17th century tragedies, several of which are represented in this book. You, the actor, must live in the play's world and commit to it. Your prime objective is to tell the truth about your character, whatever the play. The style of the text, whether prose, blank verse, or rhymed couplets, is simply a part of that truth.

- Jan Silverman

FOR PATRICK QUINN,
LATE PRESIDENT OF ACTORS' EQUITY ASSOCIATION,
WHO DEDICATED HIS LIFE
TO THE BETTERMENT
OF HIS FELLOW ACTORS

YOUNG WOMEN'S DRAMATIC MONOLOGUES

From **Medea**, *by Euripides*

Adapted by Freyda Thomas

(Her answer to her soon to be ex-husband Jason's reasonable suggestion that she let bygones be bygones and just disappear quietly, so he can remarry.)

MEDEA.

You sniv'ling coward! Let me shout it out,
So none who hear me will have any doubt
That you are not a man, not in the least!
One could not hold you to the lowest beast
In all the land! Reproach you? Listen well,
For you deserve the hottest fires of hell
For what you've done to me. But after all,
In the grand scheme of things, they were but small,
The sacrifices I have made for you.
Of course, your people know, and give me due,
But you've forgotten all. The per'lous trip
Aboard the Argo, how I saved that ship,
And killed the snake that guards the Golden Fleece
So you could ride in triumph back to Greece,
But what was that? The merest little task,
A tiny favor anyone might ask,
As though I'd merely begged to shake your hand.
And what of my betrayal of the land
That bore and raised me? Yes, I turned my back
On father, fatherland. How does that stack
Against the joys you've given me? 'Tis naught.
What insignificance that I have brought
You thither to the land of Pelias,
And organized a stunning coup de grace.

All saw him killed by his own daughters' hands,
So you might have the ruling of his lands.
A joke! And my reward? You take a bride,
And I and our two children are denied.
I'm lost. Where can I go? Back to my home,
My father? I think not. No, I must roam
The earth and tell the tale of treachery
To all who listen. Bound in beggary
By him I saved. Oh, God, you should well mark
Men's bodies with a sign. This one is dark
Of heart. You must avoid him at all cost.
Look for the noble man or you are lost.

*From **Medea**, by Euripides*

Adapted by Freyda Thomas

(The child killer of ancient times tells the Greek Chorus of her plan.)

MEDEA.

Oh, God of justice, light of Helios!
No piteous tears, no gestures lachrymose!
'Tis time for action! Enemies forebode,
The die is cast–my foot is on the road.
I'm confident. They'll pay the heavy price
And tremble at the dreaded sacrifice.
Yea, I shall triumph! Aigeus* has proved
That in my plight a man's heart can be moved.
To him I go, but not until such deeds
As satisfy this scornèd woman's needs.
So, let me tell you of my simple plan.
A servant will I send to find the man,
My husband, Jason. Will he come to me
But once more? When he does, there will he see
A softly spoken wife. I'll tell him, "Yes,
I understand your choice, in fact I bless
The union you have made. Though I am scorned,
I have accepted my cruel fate and mourned.
But"—here I'll beg—"my children. Keep them here.
Though in a land which hates me, I would fear
To leave them, yet I know you will protect
Them well." And then, with def'rence and respect
I'll send those children on a little visit
To see the lovely bride-to-be. Exquisite,
The gifts they bear. A finely woven gown,
And for her regal head, a jeweled crown.
Such generosity, you say? I say as well,
That such a gift will send her straight to hell,
For such a poison have I smeared inside
The dress, that when the vain and greedy bride
Shall put it on, and poison touch her skin,
That very night the torture shall begin.
How sad that I am forced to such a deed,

*(AY—gee-us)

But justified it is, you must concede.
Her death is my redemption, is it not?
As to the second chapter of the plot,
The words I cannot utter without tears…
My children must be killed. Their tender years
Cut short by my own hand-no! I must do it,
Though curst I'll be, for all will misconstrue it.
Their lives, you know, are worthless from this day,
No haven safe enough. So he must pay
For his own treachery with their two lives.
Such is the lot of men who leave their wives.
And when I've brought his house down with this flood
Of vengeance, I shall flee and leave their blood
To sour the rivers of this cursèd place.
My enemies I will not deign to face,
But cast myself adrift upon a sea
Of guilt and shame. This torture comes to me
For having left my precious father's house
And taken him who spurns me for a spouse.
Well, so be it. Now, childless shall he be,
And wifeless, but forever he'll have me
To think upon, the meek, obedient wife
Who acquiesced, then took away his life,
But left him to endure the endless pain
Of memory. Husband, this is your domain,
I pray you watch it burn to its last ember,
And at the end, it's I you will remember.

*From **Antigone**, by Sophocles*

Adapted by Jan Silverman

(Creon, the new ruler in Thebes, is trying to restore order to the city, after the end of a bloody civil war, fought between Eteocles and Polyneices [sons of former king Oedipus]. Both sons have died in battle. Creon, for political reasons, has decided that Eteocles was a hero and Polyneices a traitor, and his corpse must be left to rot, unburied, on a hillside. This edict contradicts religious law, since an unburied person's soul would never rest, but would suffer eternally. Antigone, the sister of both dead brothers, defies Creon's order and buries her brother, digging a hole in the ground with her hands. The penalty for such an offense is death. Antigone speaks this monologue as she sits walled in a cave by Creon.)

ANTIGONE.

Here is the place where I must end my life—
A prison and a bridal chamber too.
I wanted so much more. I hoped for love,
And children, but I feel the pull of all
My dead ones. I'm the last, and now it's time
To join them, without really having lived.
My mother and my father—will I be
Welcomed by you, be safe in your embrace?
I poured out sweet libations on your tombs
And now I need your sweetness. And for you,
My dearest brothers, I have done the most,
And paid the most. Especially for you,
My Polyneices, for I did you honors,
And for those honors, I am paid with shame.
I wonder whether I will be remembered
As one who did her duty, even though
The law says I was wrong. And even now,
When I look back, I stand amazed to think
That courage filled my soul. To think I dared!
If Polyneices were to me a husband,
I wouldn't have defied my country's law;
And even for my children, if I had them,

I could not dare so much. For after all,
I could have had more children, or a new
Sweet mate. But Polyneices, I could never have
Another brother! Our dead parents left
Us to each other only. So I dared,
And honored you beyond all sense or safety,
Knowing that Creon's punishment would come.
Now I'm alone, without a friend for comfort.
I'll never marry, never know the love
Of children or a husband. But I know
The meaning of despair. God, help me now!
My courage curst as insolence, my deed
Of love proclaimed as criminal! Dear God,
If you approve my punishment, I will
Accept this bitter death. But bitterer
I would not wish on those who bring me down.

*From **Hercules**, by Euripides*

Adapted by Freyda Thomas

(**NOTE:** *This is Euripides' variation on the Greek myth of Heracles, about his life after marriage to Megara and the siring of their children. Leaving his wife and three sons in Thebes, he goes to Argos on a mission. Completing the assignment, he descends to Hades, spends a long time there and then returns, much to the surprise of everyone. In the midst of a Civil War against Megara's father, [Creon, who currently rules in Thebes,] lycus is able to seize power and sentence Megara and her sons to death to protect his throne. Here she pleads for her life.)*

MEGARA.

Old sire; who once led our men to battle,
And who destroyed the Taphians where they dwelt,[2]
Tell me, why are so dark the ways of God
Toward men? I had prosperity—a home,
A father blessed with wealth and family,
Who gave me in such noble marriage to
The mighty Heracles, who now lies dead,[3]
As you and I, old man, shall likewise be.
And worse, these babes who nestle in my arms
And cry incessantly, "Where is our father?
What is he doing? When shall he return?"
I tell them stories, but at every sound
They jump and run to look at who approaches.
What hope have we, old man, what chance to save
Ourselves, or be saved? We have only you,
Your agéd wits must help us, set us free.
How do we slip from sentries on the road?
Where are the friends on whom we counted, where?
Please tell me if you have conceived a plan
Or must we all resign ourselves to death?

Definitions and notes:
1 Old sire: Amphitryon, Megara's father-in-law
2 Taphians:) Natives of Taphiae, a group of islands in the Ionian Sea.
3 Heracles:): son of Zeus and Alcmene, a princess of Mycenae

*From **Hercules**, by Euripides*

Adapted by Freyda Thomas

(**NOTE:** *For an explanation of this character's situation, see preceding monologue.*)

MEGARA.

Where is the priest who wields the sharpened sword?
Where is this slayer of my precious sons?
Incongruous death, come now, come unto us.
But let me look one moment more upon
The dearest faces ever known to me.
I filled my belly with your souls, and brought
You to this world, just long enough to see
The hope I founded on your father's words
Turn bitterly to ash beneath our feet.

(*To one son.*)

All Argos was to be your sweet domain.[1]
You would have ruled in stately marble halls,
And held the reins in rich Pelasgia.[2]
You know, your father wore a lion skin,
Which he upon occasion would enfold
Around your tiny body as you slept.

(*To another son.*)

And you, the true and rightful king of Thebes,[3]
My lands were to be yours and yours alone.

(*To all her sons.*)

Did you know I had chosen brides as well
For you? A maid of Athens, one of Thebes,
A third from Sparta.[4] Happiness you would
Have known with three such noble maids. But now,
All is to ashes, gone. Good fortune turns
And gives you death to lead you by the hand.

1 Argos: A city in Southeast Greece.
2 Pelasgia: The region in antiquity that covered Greece, Asia Minor and the islands of the eastern Mediterranean.
3 Thebes: A very powerful city state throughout Greek history, situated northeast of Athens.
4 Sparta: Located in South Greece, known for its training of warriors.

Which one must I embrace the first? The last?
Oh, blessèd Heracles,[5] if any voice
Can pierce the earth to Hades where you dwell,
Please hear me now! Your sons, your father, I,
All marked for death. Come back to us! A spectre
In a dream would give us peace–a ghost
To frighten those who would destroy your sons!

---

5 *Heracles: part mortal, part god.*

*From **Iphigenia at Aulis**, by Euripides*

Adapted by Jan Silverman

(Poor Iphigenia. Depending on who's telling the story, either her own father sacrifices her to Artemis, goddess of the winds, so he can sail to Troy and get Helen back, or her mother, Clytemnestra, whisks her away and puts a deer in her place and she goes to Taurus to become a priestess. Euripides wrote both stories—see monologues from Iphigenia at Taurus—but in this one she thinks the axe is about to descend and implores her father to spare her life.)

IPHIGENIA.

Dear father, if I only had the gift
Of Orpheus, whose voice can charm the rocks,
I'd use it now to try to melt your heart.
But all I have are tears. I'm on my knees—
I beg you not to kill me! I'm too young
To journey to that dark and fearsome place
Beneath the earth. Dear father, I'm your child,
Your first born. You would hold me on your lap,
And kiss me sweetly, and I'd kiss you back.
You'd tell me how you'd one day see me married,
The happy bride of a most worthy husband!
And I'd tell you that, in that far-off day,
When you grew old, I'd joyfully receive you
As you had cared for me. Have you forgot?
I hear our words so clearly even now.
But you have stopped your ears and closed your heart,
And say you want to kill me! In the name
Of Atreus, your father, spare my life!
And for my mother's sake, who suffered long
To give me birth, I pray you, spare my life!
That evil Helen! How is it my fault
That Paris took her off? What's he to me,
Or I to them? It makes no sense! I beg
You, look at me! Please, kiss me, smile at me,
Let me at least remember at my death
That you still love me.

*(Bringing her baby brother **Orestes** forward.)*

                               Little brother, please
Come help me now. Plead for me to our father,
And shed your tears for my sake. Father, see?
Even a baby has a sense of sorrow.
My brother weeps for me. Can you do less?
Dear father, life is sweet, and death is darkness.
I'm so afraid of that great nothingness,
That void, that night, oh, please don't send me there!
Chastise me if you must, revile me, beat me!
Even an evil and unhappy life
Is better than the awful gloom of death!

*From **Iphigenia at Taurus**, by Euripides*

Adapted by Jan Silverman

(In this version of the story, Iphigenia is in exile in Taurus, after the mysterious sacrifice at Aulis, where a deer, slain in her place, has saved her life. Here she muses on the downfall of her family, past joys and what she has lost. This play, unlike most Greek tragedies, could be considered a romance, as it ends in redemption. For further backstory, check Iphigenia's other monologue in this volume.)

IPHIGENIA.

My family is gone. Our very name—
Atreides*—once lit the world with glory.
But now our light is out. My father's house[1]
Has crumbled, and its ruins break my heart.
My father's fathers, ancient kings of Argos,
Where is your kingdom now? Where do you reign?
Wild steeds of sorrow gallop over us
And grind us into dust. What awful deeds
Have so repelled the sun to turn his face
And shine on us no more? Our family
Was golden once, and loved in Thessaly.
That gold has tarnished. Murder and revenge[1]
Brought grief and acts of horror, endless woes,
And from the countless dead, vengeance arose
And in its rushing tide swept us away.
And we, offspring of Tantalus, are gone.
My doom was sealed the moment that my mother
Lay down upon her bridal bed. And from
That night, when she conceived me, unkind Fate
Has been my nursemaid. Even though my mother
Is Leda's daughter, even though I have
The honor to be first-born, I am doomed
Upon the order of the king, my father,
To be the victim in a sacrifice.
I was so happy once. I can remember

1 This refers to the old tale of Atreus, who served his brother Thyestes a banquet, featuring a tasty dish composed of his own children. Iphigenia's father, Agamemnon, and her uncle, Aegisthes, who becomes her mother's lover, are the descendants of these ancient enemies, still battling it out.
(a-TREE-uh-deez)

The day I came to Aulis, wrapped in love.
The son of Thetis chose me for his bride,
Preferring me to all the Grecian beauties.
I glowed with pride and happiness that day.
How life has changed! A stranger and alone,
I creep along this barren shore, so far
From home, and all that I held dear. I'll have
No wedding day, no bridal night, no lover;
No children, friends or family. I'm lost.
I'll never see again my home in Argos,
I'll never sing our songs in Juno's[2] praise,
Or work upon my loom. Oh, how I loved
Creating tapestries alive with color,
Forming ferocious Titans with my threads
Of silk, shaping Athena in the act
Of throwing her vermillion spear. My work
Is ended now. Alone, I sit, so idle
In this savage country. I've seen horrors,
Watched sacrifices, heard the groans and screams
And seen the blood spilled out upon the altar.
For every tear I see, I shed one too.
My grief is greatest in the memory
Of my dead brother[3]—sharpest pain of all.
He looked so beautiful the day I left him,
Sweetly asleep, safe in his mother's arms.
Secure, I thought, his destiny to reign
In Argos—blesséd future king! And now
He too goes down to join the dead. His loss
Of all the other losses is the worst.

2 *The highest goddess in heaven, the Roman name for Hera, wife of Zeus.*
3 *Orestes, who isn't really dead but she doesn't know it.*

From **Helen**, *by Euripides*

Adapted by Freyda Thomas

(This play takes place in Egypt, near the mouth of the Nile and in front of the royal house. The tomb of King Proteus is downstage. Helen sits next to the tomb speaking to the chorus of wise women. The husband she speaks of is Menelaus. Helen is, of course, the infamous Helen of Troy, who caused the Trojan War. This takes place long after that debacle.)

HELEN.

What is this destiny to which I'm called?
Tell me, wise women, friends, am I a monster?
Born of great Zeus and Leda, so they say,[1]
The sinful deed that curses all my days.
Or yet, my beauty, which I never loved
Nor wanted, caused such horror that I pray[2]
To be redone, in plainer tones. Had I
Been thus created, who would know of Helen?
No Greek would cry of my misfortune—no!
They curse me—all imagined wrongs—yet I
Did nothing to engender it. No kin
Have I, torn cruelly from my home and brought
To this barbarian land. A slave am I,
Though once born free. I had one single hope:
My husband might one day deliver me.
And now that hope is vanished with his life.
My mother died, my daughter will grow old,
Unmarried. So my fortune turns to grief.
I walk and see and hear, yet I am dead.
Both dead and living, why do I go on?
Could I not marry a barbarian?
Sit down at tables richly laden? No,
I think death better company. To die
By rope or knife or some such other means,
That is the destiny of desperate queens.

---

1 *Great Zeus and Leda: Zeus was the king of the gods*
2 *"Caused such horror": The Trojan War.*

*From **Hecuba**, by Euripides*

Adapted by Freyda Thomas

(This is Polyxena's response to Odysseus, who may spare her life.)

POLYXENA.
Your hand, Odysseus, couched between the folds
Of your most kingly robes. Your face you hide,
For fear that I may meet your eyes, imploring
You to spare my life. Be not afraid,
I shall not call great Zeus to help my cause,
I shall not beg for life. I long to die.
So, freely do I go with you. I must.
To live would be to prove myself a coward.
I am a princess of the blood, once nourished
On hope that I would be a bride for Kings,
And great example to the maids of Troy,
Who smiled at princes begging for my hand;
Great mistress. Yes, and courted, near to goddess,
But now, a slave; foul, ugly name, and strange,
A sound that makes me long for noble death.
Should I not die, and thus be sold for cash,
To some cruel master? Hector's sister bonded,
Kneading bread, and scrubbing filthy floors?
No respite from the endless dreary days?
Bone weary, tossed upon some straw at night
For some slave's lusty satisfaction? Never.
My eyes are free to look away from life,
Renouncing light and casting toward the dark
O, soul, so welcome is that goddess, Death.

*From **Don Juan**, by Molière*

Translated and adapted by Freyda Thomas

(This is arguably Molière's most serious play, and since Don Juan ends up in the fires of hell, it could be considered a tragedy. Yet there are comic elements, coming mostly from Sganarelle, his servant and by the time this was written, a recognizable figure in Molière's theatre canon. In this monologue, Don Juan's latest cast-off returns in the darkness of night and in disguise to forgive the man she loves and beg him to change his evil ways. This is one of Molière's prose plays.)

DONA ELVIRA.

Ah, you're surprised to see me, so late and dressed like this. I had to come. It couldn't wait. No, I'm not angry—not any more. Not like I was this morning. All that bitterness, that overwhelming desire to avenge you for your unspeakable behavior toward me—it's gone. I prayed and prayed on it, all day, and finally, as the dark crept into the sky, the light crept into my soul. I love you, now more completely, more truly than ever I did before, when lust and desire were coursing through my veins. When we love purely, we want only the happiness and safety of the object of our love. And so I came to you, with a full knowledge of all the transgressions, the mistakes, the selfish choices you have made in your life. I think I could name every one—could you? Have you thought once about the consequences of your actions? I don't mean what they have done to others, but what they have done to you? What they are doing and will continue to do? Do you see the path you are on and where it's leading? I can't go from you and forge a new life without at least trying to warn you—to stop you if I can, to beg you to turn from this treacherous road that seals your heart away from all human goodness. No one in the world is dearer to me than you, no one have I loved more. If you ever had any feeling for me at all, I beg you, change the direction your soul has taken. If you love yourself, if you ever loved me, save yourself. Save yourself. Save yourself.

*From **Nana**, by Emile Zola*

*(**Nana**, 30's, a once-famous Paris courtesan is at the end of her rope, used up and dissipated by Paris society in the 19th century. Her lover, Zizi, has just died and Nana has just been informed of it. She speaks to a Friend, who is listening to her lament.)*

NANA.

Dead!? Zizi is dead!? Oh, mon Dieu, mon Dieu, have pity on me! I am a wretched soul. A miserable, wretched, wicked woman! That's what they'll all call me—that mother who is grieving for her son, the poor fool who moaned outside my door this morning, all the others who ruined themselves because of me, all their money gone! Voilà. Blame it all on Nana. Everything's always my fault. Can't you hear them already in the streets? Nana is a dirty whore who beds with anyone, she ruins some men and kills the rest! She makes everybody unhappy...(*She sobs.*), oh, it hurts, it hurts so bad! It's choking me! It's too painful, to be so misunderstood, to watch people turn on you because they're stronger. But why is it my fault? Why? No, by God, no. No matter what they say! Have I ever been cruel? Haven't I given away everything I had? Don't they remember I was always nice to them? They hung on to my skirts like little beggars, and that's what they've become. Dirty little beggars. All dying or begging and in despair...(*To friend.*) You were here. You saw everything. Did I lead them on? Didn't they all clamor to see me? Did I ever encourage them? No. Never. They disgusted me. Yet they would have stolen, murdered even, just to marry me. And this is my reward. Look at Daguenet. I kept him for weeks when he had no money and no place to go, arranged a profitable marriage for him, set him up in the world. Yesterday I saw him on the street and he looked the other way! It's not fair, it's not fair! Society's all wrong. Women get blamed when it's men who demand things. You want to know something? All those men I was with? I never enjoyed it. Not once. It bored me. It disgusted me! If it hadn't been for them and what they made me I'd be in a convent praying right now, dressed in long black robes and lighting candles for mass.

*From **Hecuba**, by Euripides*

Adapted by Freyda Thomas

(Talthybius, a herald of the Greeks, brings the message from Agamemnon of the death of Hecuba's daughter. **NOTE:** *This is a cross-gender monologue, for a man or woman.)*

TALTHYBIUS.

How can I tally such a cost in telling
This fierce tale, oh Hecuba, my queen?
Tears blur the vision of your daughter's death,
And more will cloud my eyes before I end
My woeful story. All the army stood
At strict attention waiting, watching, silent,
As poor Polyxena came through the camp.
Achilles' son led her, with troops behind,
They marched in great procession to the tomb.
Once in their place, Odysseus raised a goblet,
Drank a toast to great Achilles' spirit,
And said, "Oh, ghost of my departed father,
Take offerings to raise your spirit high.
This virgin's blood, as fresh and pure as snow,
We give to you. Be gracious now to us,
Set free our ships and bring us home from Troy."
Thus praying, he then grasped his deadly sword
And signaled to the guards to seize your child,
But she said, "Wait, you Greeks who came and sacked
My city: of my own free will I die,
But let no man restrain me like a slave.
I offer up my throat. I will not flinch.
So, I must die as one of royal blood."
And, saying thus, she sank upon her knees,
Raised up her head, so beauteous in the light,
Then rent her robes, and bared her virgin breasts,
Which glowed like marble in the blinding sun.
Well I could see upon the face of he,
Who held her fate within his hands, the horror
Of the deed he had to do. The sword

Was raisèd high, and with one perfect blow,
Her throat was cut, her blood began to flow,
And she, with grace, fell dying on the pyre.
So, now you know it as it was revealed
To all who did observe. Your daughter died
The noblest, bravest death I e'er have seen,
Both blest and curst are you to know that she
Brought honor to your house upon her end.

*From **Electra**, by Euripides*

Adapted by Freyda Thomas

(Electra, brought down by her mother and sent to live with a poor farmer, begs a stranger, whom she doesn't recognize as her brother, Orestes, to tell her brother of her troubles:)

ELECTRA.
I beg you, tell my brother of my woe:
All great misfortune to me he must know.
Tell him I dress in rags, a stable beast
To fetch and carry, how my skin is greased
And dirty from the toil I must endure.
This is his sister, who was once so pure.
Describe to him this hovel called my home,
This filthy hair that sees no soothing comb,
My fingers bleed from toiling at the loom,
Tell him this bleakness is my fate—my doom.
I danced at festivals not long ago,
Conversed with well-born women. Now they know
Me not, yet mother sits upon her throne,
While many serve her whim. I sit alone,
Far from her wickedness, far from the mud
Around her palace, stained with father's blood.
Oh, father,[1] goodly man, your murderer
Now drives your chariot and beds with her
You once called wife. He flaunts his name
In drunken revel, and fills yours with shame.
"Orestes! Come protect your father's tomb!"
He cries, the monster who ordained your doom.
He spits upon your grave, pelts it with stones
As if to break apart your precious bones.
And still my brother does not come. Go tell
Him of this dark despair, this living hell
In which we wait for him to come and right
The wrong that plunges us in endless night.

1 *Agamemnon, who is dead*

*From **Andromache**, by Euripides*

Adapted by Freyda Thomas

(The opening speech of the play, explaining the back-story. Andromache enters and sits at the foot of a statue, where she is attempting to gain sanctuary.)

ANDROMACHE.

Oh, Thetis, help this wretched soul you see
Before you. I am called Andromache,
Once wife of Hector, envied in past days,
Now I am called the strumpet who betrays.
No woman's life e'er held such bitterness.
All whom I loved, all that I did possess,
Great wealth, nobility, all turned to dust
In that horrific siege of Troy. Unjust
It has to be that I should see my son
Thrown to his death from such a height. Well done,
You Greeks. My husband, killed before my eyes
By great Achilles sword. And I the prize,
Brought as a concubine upon this shore,
The spoils of Troy. Ah, Fate, all this I bore
In silence. And I bore a son as well,
My master's son. Within this citadel
We lived, I with the hope that he, one day,
Would mend my shattered life and find a way
To end my boundless misery. But now,
Another great misfortune won't allow
My rescue or my retribution. She,
The heinous creature called Hermione,
Who wed my master and is barren still,
Thinks me to blame, thinks I have wished her ill
And curst her womb. Her husband tires of her,
And she believes 'tis I he would prefer,
And I who have bewitched him. 'Tis not so!
I've come for sanctuary, I'll not go!
Protect me from her wrath, protect my son
Whom I have sent away, lest he's undone
By her, or worse, her father, who has come
To help her in her wild delerium.

And he, the object of this tale of woe,
My master and her husband, does not know
That she would murder us. He's gone away
To Delphi to atone for sins and pray,
And I am left without a single friend.
Oh, Thetis, tell me soon, how this will end!?

*From **Andromache**, by Jean Racine*

Adapted by Freyda Thomas

*(In this 17th century version of the Greek tragedy, Hermione has asked Orestes, who is madly in love with her, to kill Pyrrhus, with whom she is madly in love, because Pyrrhus loves his captive slave, Andromache. Talk about tragedy, this is a no-win situation for everybody. If Andromache doesn't marry Pyrrhus, he'll kill her son whose father was slain by the very man who wants to marry her. Everybody's in love with everybody else and ready to kill to get what they want. Just another normal day in Ancient Greece or 17th century France. **NOTE:** In the French version of this Greek tragedy, Andromache is pronounced "ahn-dro-mack," with equal emphasis on all syllables.)*

HERMIONE.
What have I done, oh Gods, what have I done?!
What madness seizes me, what grief devours?
I wander, lost within this frigid palace,
Not knowing even if I love or hate.
His eyes, his eyes,[1] oh, cruelty! With one look
I was dismissed. And he shed not a tear!
No furrowed brow, no sympathetic sigh.
Untouched, he stood there, watching my eyes spill
With pain so long suppressed. "'Tis not my doing,"
He must have thought, his placid face a mask.
Oh, wretched am I! And made more so by
My heart which echoes one long cry: I love!
I love him[2] still and fear for him. I quake
To think that he's been threatened. Sweet revenge,
You should be mine, and yet I want you not!
No, let him die. Let judgment not be stayed.
Triumphant, he cares not for me, believes
A storm of tears will dissipate my rage,
His past perception of me. Look again!
Be not distracted in your temple, sir,
Look to your life or death. I am uncertain,

1 *Pyrrhus' eyes*
2 *Pyrrhus*

But hear me well, I'll let Orestes act![3]
'Tis he, yes, he, who forces me to wish
For such an end. I wish? Do I ordain
This death out of my love for that fair prince,
Whose brilliant deeds with such delight I told?
How can I—no, I must. He is too cruel.
He stands upon the hill, proud conqueror,
With Andromache beside him, seeing nothing
But her face. False heart! Gods, let him die!

3 kill Pyrrhus

From **Phedre**, by Jean Racine

Adapted by Freyda Thomas

(The beautiful, young and innocent Aricia, who, in war, has been taken captive by King Aegisthis, has fallen in love with Hippolyte, his son, and he with her. All would normally be well, if not for Phedre, wife to Theseus, who happens to be bonkers for her stepson. She speaks to her companion, Oenone.)

ARICIA

What precious words now fall upon my ears?
Hippolytus loves me? O, God, my heart
Hears what you say, but fears that this must be
A wisp of smoke, a cloud without foundation.
It cannot be. You, who observe my fate:
I am a dog, whose nourishment has been
A feast of bitter tears and heavy anguish.
How could a creature such as I gain love
With all its foolish agonies? The sole
Survivor of a king, great son of earth,
Who fell in war where I did not? I rose
From singéd ashes as six brothers perished!
Thus, scorned and shunned, none dared to love the spoil,
Lest vengeance come from those inhuman deeds
That took their lives and spared but mine. And, too,
I viewed love with severity, suspicion.
Alas, my eyes had not beheld this man,
Hippolytus, his father's son in strength,
So much alike, and yet so unalike.
How rash am I, so humbled in defeat
To love the conqueror who binds my chains?
I love, I love, and would make captive him
Whose father slew my kin. How can this be?
Yet, humbled in defeat my soul cries out,
Hippolytus loves me, and heaven's mine!

*From **Electra,** by Hugo von Hofmanstal*

Adapted by Freyda Thomas

*(In this version, Chrysothemis, Electra's sister, is living
in poverty with her, a kind of self-imposed exile that Electra has forced her sister to bear with her, in protest of her
father's murder. Chrysothemis has had enough!)*

CHRYSOTHEMIS.

Oh, sister, I cannot sit in that dark
Foreboding place, like you. My heart is burning,
And I roam the house incessantly.
I climb the stairs, come down again, for peace
Is not within that place. I choose a room
And think it may bring comfort to this angst.
But, after all it is an empty room
That stares at me with empty, lifeless eyes,
Like father's, and I rush to quit the space,
My knees a-tremble, clutching at my throat
For tears to be released that will not come.
I'm turning into stone—have pity on me!
'Tis you who put me in this wretched state,
For if not for your rage we would be free,
Not locked and chained within this horrid place.
I must, I will get out! I'll not sleep here
Each cold and endless night 'til I am dead.
I want to know what life is! 'Ere I'm old,
I want to feel a babe kick in my womb,
Though they may choose a beggar for my mate.
I'll bear him children, warm him on cold nights,
As raging storms howl round our hovel. No!
No more this living hell! Who stands to gain
From such a bleak condition? Father's dead,
He's dead! And sweet Orestes[1] does not come.
Day after day, no news of him at all!
I'll die before I'll live another day
Like this, wasting away, losing my soul.

---

1 *The brother of Electra and Chrysothemis, who disappeared several years ago.
They await his return to avenge their father's death.*

*From **Electra**, by Hugo von Hofmanstal*

(In this German version of the Greek tragedy, Electra speaks to her father's dead spirit, begging him to come back and tell her what to do to avenge his murder.)

ELECTRA.

Where are you, father? Summon all your power
And come again to earth—time is at hand,
This is our time—come now to me, I beg you!
Think of the moment when the knives went in
And you were slaughtered—think of that cold hour.
Think on your wife, the harlot in her bed,
Your bed now shared by your most cruel assassin.
Remember how the bath you sat in ran
With blood—the water steamed with it, and then
The monster dragged you from the bloody chamber,
Head first, your legs so white with ebbing life,
Your wounds agape, your eyes in a blank stare,
Oh please, my father, think upon this horror
And come back to avenge the dog who stole
Your life, your family and your kingdom. Father!
Don't leave me here alone to bear this pain,
Show me your spirit, if but just a shadow,
There, within the niche, like yesterday-
Come back—your time is coming—all the stars
Do signal it—one hundred slashèd throats
Will cleanse your grave and we, your son and daughters,
We three, when all is well avenged, shall stand
'Neath royal canopies and dance for joy
Around your tomb and over bloody corpses.
And all who see the spectacle shall say
How great this king was who is celebrated
By his own flesh and blood, there at his grave.

*From **Antigone**, by Sophocles*

Adapted by Jan Silverman

(Here, Antigone is caught red-handed burying her brother. She answers Creon's charge that she has broken the law. For a fuller overview of the story, see Antigone's previous monologue.)

ANTIGONE.
The law! What law? *Your* law. You're not a god.
And Justice doesn't flow from mortal rules.
How dare you say your edict, which you drew
In anger, for revenge, is greater than
The law of God, created for all time?
I'm not afraid to answer for my deed
To God. And I am not afraid of you!
I know the penalty. And from the first
I knew that you would have me killed for this.
But don't expect that I'll beg for my life
Or tremble, and bow down before your power.
So do your worst! For what is life to me?
A long nightmare of horror, death and loss.
No! I have no regrets. But, if I'd failed
To bury my poor brother, then regret
Would overcome me. You believe I'm wrong.
Your pride won't let you bend, or even hear me,
Because your pride has stopped your ears, and made you
Deaf to the truth. But you will hear the truth
One day, the day it strikes you down.

From **Cyrano de Bergerac**, *by Edmond Rostand*

Adapted by Freyda Thomas

(The beautiful young Roxane, loved secretly by the nose-bound Cyrano, has traveled to see young, handsome Christian, the man she thinks she loves. Unbeknownst to her, Cyrano has been writing letters and signing Christian's name and she has fallen in love with the wrong man.)

ROXANE.

Oh, Christian, 'tis your fault I have come here
And braved the danger. 'Twas for you, my dear.
Your poetry, your heart would drive me mad
For one sweet glimpse of you. Are you not glad?
Your letters, like your voice that silvered night
Beneath my window, cast such shimm'ring light
Into my soul, that, throwing fear aside,
I faced the blackened woods and dared to ride,
To be with you this one night! How could I,
Receiving such sweet words not glorify
The man who wrote them? Twenty times I read
Each one, and gave myself to you. I fed
Upon their beauty, every page a feast.
Yet more I read, the more the flame increased,
Until I knew my love for you had grown
To that sweet place where you and you alone—
Your true self, yes, your soul, was what I love,
Nay, not your sweetest face, but worship of
The purest soul I've ever seen. How vain
Was I to love the shell. 'Tis like a stain
Upon my honor to confess my sin,
And you, my love, how sad you must have been
To think my love so shallow. 'Tis not true.
Why, were you ugly, I should still love you.

*From **Phedre**, by Jean Racine*

Adapted by Freyda Thomas

(Married to Theseus a short time, Phedre meets his son Hippolytus and falls truly, madly, deeply in love with him. She tells her companion how it happened.)

PHEDRE.

How can I tell you when it all began?
Believe me, trusted friend, I did not plan
The thing. Great gods, I barely was the wife
Of Theseus! And we had a happy life
Ahead of us, so peaceful and secure.
My heart was light, my love for him was pure,
Then came the trip to Athens and I saw
My enemy, my torment, and a claw
Clutched round my heart. I'd see him and turn pale,
Then blush, my mind would fog, my speech would fail,
My blood run cold, then turn to searing fire—
I could not stop this feverish desire!
That vixen Venus followed everywhere.
The marketplace, the temple, she was there.
The louder I protested, th'more I prayed
For respite from my pain, the more she stayed
And whispered in my ear, incessantly,
"You love his son. You cannot let him be,
But must pursue this vile villainy."
I shunned him, sent him from me in disgrace,
Only to find him in his father's face.
So I became the shrew. I persecuted,
Made sure his father's mind was well polluted
With lies about his son, until his heart
Was hardened and the two were forced to part.
I breathed again, for quite a while, it seemed,
Submitted to my husband's will, and dreamed
Of finding some tranquility of mind.
I prayed again to Venus, "Make me blind
To this base passion, tame this heart so wild!"
And then, he and my husband reconciled,

And I am worse now than I was before.
I am a soldier, constantly at war,
Forced to do battle with a heavy chain
Wound round me. I shall surely go insane.

*From **Antigone**, by Sophocles*

Adapted by Jan Silverman

(Ismene, the younger sister of Antigone, knows of her intention to break the law and bury their brother. She sympathizes with her but fears the death penalty Creon will declare. For further backstory, see Antigone's other monologues in this volume.)

ISMENE.

Dear Sister, please—you're all that I have left.
Remember our poor father's bitter fate
Discov'ring his own guilt and stabbing out
His weeping eyes. And then our mother chose
To hang herself, she couldn't find a way
To live with what she knew. Her gentle touch
Will never come again. Our brothers fought
And died, denying us the grace of their
Protection. We're alone! We're what remains
From Oedipus' misbegotten kin.
And we'll die too if we transgress the law.
Antigone, he means it, Creon means it!
He won't have mercy on us, any more
Than if we had been strangers. He's the king!
And we're but subjects. Leave the men to fight!
We're only women! What else can we do?
I'm praying to our dead ones to forgive me,
But I'll obey the edict of the king.
And you must too, Antigone, I beg you!
Your plan's ridiculous! You go too far.
Don't meddle in affairs beyond your power!

MATURE WOMEN'S DRAMATIC MONOLOGUES

*From **Medea**, by Euripides*

Adapted by Freyda Thomas

(This is the opening speech of the play, establishing the plot.)

NURSE.

Love is diseased within this house. Cruel fate
Has turned Medea's passion into hate,
As piteous cries I hear behind her walls,
And pacing, pacing up and down the halls.
She takes no food or drink, her suffering
These last days is a sickly, sorrowed thing.
Yet justly so, when one hears of the story
Of Jason and Medea and their glory.
Her glory, should I say, and how she came
To help him in his quest, so all would name
Him hero, taker of the Golden Fleece.
Renowned he is for that through all of Greece.
Oh, why did Argo's wingèd oars cut through
The fjords of Colchis, skimming o'er the blue
Symplegades[1] to fetch that cursèd fleece?
My lady would this day be left in peace,
Safe in her homeland. She would ne'er have sailed
To Iolcus[2], nor have seen her heart impaled
By Jason's sting. Would she have cast a spell
On Peleas' daughters, now in hell
Because she bade them murder their own father?
Would any of this cause her such a bother
As Jason's cruel betrayal of her love?
Ah, for a time it seemed she'd rise above
All censure. Here in Corinth, where they came,

1 sim-PLEH-ga-deez
2 YOL-KUS

She was respected. Now they mock her name,
And how my lady suffers! Jason weds
Another. Can he occupy two beds?
Nay. And my lady's is the one he spurns,
For whom? The daughter of a king. She burns
With agony and rage. She cannot eat,
Lies limp upon her bed in mute defeat,
Eyes to the floor, as though some object there
Might make her soon forget her deep despair.
No friend can bring her sympathy. She hears
No voice. At times she looks up and appears
To see her father. Then she moans and cries,
Tears at her clothes, throws curses to the skies.
Her sons she cannot bear to look upon,
For she sees Jason in them. Reason gone,
She has become, I fear, a danger to
I know not what, nor where, nor when, nor who.

*From **Iphigenia**, by Jean Racine*

Adapted by Freyda Thomas

*(In this 17th century interpretation of the Greek tragedy, the gods tell Agamemnon, father of Iphigenia, that she must be sacrificed to appease the angered Greeks. Her mother, Clytemnestra, takes a stand against his agonized decision. **NOTE:** for further backstory, see Iphigenia's monologues.)*

CLYTEMNESTRA.

Oh, truly you're a credit to your race
Of child killers![1] You will not disgrace
Your lineage with this noble sacrifice.
My daughter's butcher stands before me. Slice
Her up and serve her to me as you planned,
Please! No remorse. Perhaps you'd like a hand?
Barbarian! No horror at this deed
Consumes you? Will not tenderness impede
This fate you have endorsed? Where are your tears,
Your pity as her condemnation nears?
Tell me, where is your eloquent resistance,
Or shall you simply bow to Fate's insistence?
You love her well, you say. Well, have you tried
To save her in its name, or does your pride
Forbid you begging for her life? Oh, spare
Me all your kind concern, 'Tis false. Despair
Surrounds me! Do you know what they will do?
A priest, with his religious retinue
Will lead her through the streets, where crowds await
The bloody moment when your daughter's fate
Will free them from their curse. Then, in the square,
He'll draw his knife—will you be standing there,
Your eyes upon her face as he brings down
The blade upon her breast? I hope you drown
In all the blood she'll spill upon the road,
As he *tears out her heart* and gives what's owed

---

1 *Atreus, Agamemnon's father, to avenge himself on his brother and political rival, Thyestes (who was his wife's paramour), murdered Thyestes' children and served them up in a banquet to their father, at which horror the sun turned back on its course. Can you blame it?*

Back to the gods! I cannot let this be!
I will not see her torn away from me!
Do what you will, I will not loose my child
From my embrace, though I may be reviled
By gods and men. I swear this I shall do.
You want her life? You'll have to take mine too!

From **Electra**, *by Hugo von Hofmanstal*

Adapted by Freyda Thomas

(Clytemnestra, mother of Electra and co-murderer of her husband and Electra's father, is going just a little bonkers from the guilt of her crime, yet still refuses to admit she had a part in the deadly deed, along with her new husband, Aegisthus. Electra keeps talking of her brother Orestes, returning to avenge their father's death, a possibility that scares the devil out of Clytemnestra. In this scene, she confronts Electra, who has just taunted her about Orestes' return. She struggles to calm herself throughout the monologue, with feeble results.)

CLYTEMNESTRA.

He is not coming! Stop these worthless lies!
What do I care for someone far from here?
I live here. I am mistress of this place,
With guards aplenty watching every gate,
And if I choose, the door to my bedchamber.
So tell me any fantasy you wish,
I quite ignore your ravings. What concern
Of mine if he[1] be dead or living still?
I banish him from all my thoughts, my dreams…
Though there he is, persistent devil! Dreams
Are signs of illness. I am ill, you know,
And I must soon be cured, my strength returned,
And reign again with clarity and purpose.
I will not have this sickness! You will tell
The secrets I must know to rid my mind
Of all these nightmares! Tell me all the rites,
The sacrifices, words—I want the words!
You have a choice: to tell me willingly
Or chained within the dungeon walls. The potions,
Spells and prayers! Tell me with belly full
Or empty, starvèd, hollow-eyed and fearful.
You know the ways of emptying the mind
Of visions, haunting spectres. One can rid
Oneself of dreams, be cured, yet I cannot!

1 Orestes

What have you done to me, you wicked child!?
You've poisoned my repose, sleep never comes
But with it ghosts and voices. Stop, I say!
Oh gods, why do you let her torment me!?

YOUNG WOMEN'S COMEDIC MONOLOGUES

*From **The Princess of Elis** by Molière*

Adapted by Freyda Thomas

(In this, one of Molière's lesser plays, the love story reminds one of "Much Ado About Nothing" with the two proud lovers disdaining each other and falling more desperately in love the harder they protest. Molière was famous for stealing plots and reworking them to suit his culture.)

PRINCESS.

Oh, God, what is this feeling? This malaise
That's clutched my chest and put me in a daze?
The flu. It must be. What else could it be
That's really, truly irritating me?
It happened when I met that man. That prince.
It couldn't be—no, it's coincidence.
I need to breathe, to get my balance back.
Am I too young to have a heart attack?
My knees are weak. What an insuff'rable man!
Confusing me, that's got to be his plan,
And he's succeeded! No, he hasn't—no!
I couldn't be in love. Why, it would show
In ways much different from this. I'd sigh

(She does, not realizing that she has.)

I'd think about him and I'd start to cry...

(She does.)

But clearly that is not the case with me.
So, if it isn't love, what can it be?
Good God, the world is at my very feet!
Men gather at my door just to compete

For any crumb that I might care to throw.
Why should I care if one of them says no?
How dare he!? All that snooty condescension.
I need a drink—I can't abide this tension!

(She pours a drink, then studies the glass.)

I'm being poisoned! Someone wants me dead!
Ridiculous. I'll simply clear my head,
Breathe deeply, set my course with sense and reason.
It could be allergies—they're fierce this season!
I've never been allergic. I've been smart.
No one has ever tampered with this heart.
Why now? Why him? Ha! He despises me!
So I'll show him the same capacity.
Look right into those big blue eyes and say,
"I find you arrogant. Please go away."
No, that's too rude. "Monsieur, I find that I'm
Too busy and I haven't any time
To waste on social"—no. What would be best
To make him squirm, to make him feel…distressed.
Why, see him! Speak to him. Put on the charm.
Use flattery to weaken and disarm
The sneaky skunk. Request his company,
That ought to bring him crawling back to me,
The perfect game. But, oh, dear gods above,
Don't let him know how much I am in love!

From **The Flying Doctor** *by Molière*

Adapted by Freyda Thomas

(The no-nonsense maid explains to the ardent if not-too-swift Lelie her plan for getting him together with Lucille, his sweetheart.)

SABINE.

All right, no time to waste. With lightning speed
We have to act. First off, of course, we need...

(Making it up as she goes.)

A plan. Your heart's desire, Lucille, is ill.
No, no! Not really, we just have to kill
A little time to stall the marriage plan.
Her father—what a stupid, stubborn man—
Wants her to marry that guy Villebriquin[1]—
Briquette, whatever. Well, he's rich, you know,
So little Lucy was all set to go
And march right down the aisle and say I do,
Except, of course, the twit's in love with you,
Too. So, she's just pretending to be sick.

(Speaking through her nose.)

Her dose is stuffed, her deck has got a crick,
She's coughing, has a fever, and in fact
She's taken to her bed—no, it's an act!
Her father sent me out for medicine,
But I think I should bring a doctor in.
Somebody we can trust who'll say, "Poor dear,
She needs some rest and she won't get that here,
Fresh air and sunshine, take her there at once!"
Her father, who I've told you is a dunce,
Will fall, hook, line and sinker for the plot.
I'll take her to the country on the spot,
You'll follow, and the two of you will marry,
One two three, then forthwith I will carry
News of the event to her papá,
Who'll have a fit, then I will say, "Voilà,
It's done, there's no point getting so upset,

1 *Veel-brih-can*

However, you should go and tell Briquette,
Who's waiting at the altar. Clever plan,
N'est-ce pas[2]? Now what we need's a clever man
To play the doctor, and without delay.
Why, who's that coming? Is it your valet!?
That brilliant fellow? With those flashing eyes?
Just picture him, all decked out in disguise.
I know he's dumb as dirt, I know he's not
Too bright, but what he is, is all we've got.

1 ness-páh

*From **Sganarelle** by Molière*

Adapted by Freyda Thomas

(Molière's prototype maid pleads with her young mistress, who doesn't want to marry the man her father has chosen for her.)

MAID.

You are too obstinate, you really are,
My lady. You should thank the lucky star
That brought you such a marriage offer. Why
Do you instead tear at your clothes and cry?
You wouldn't see me carry on like this,
If someone asked for my hand. I would kiss
The fool in gratitude, for I know well
The price one pays to stay a mademoiselle,
Against the joys of being called madame.
I chose the latter title, glad I am.
When I wed Martin, heaven rest his soul,
We barely had enough to eat. No coal
To heat our hut, poor us. But I soon found
How nice it is to have a man around.
I married him the 10th of February.
Ask me if it was cold.

(She waits for a reply, gets none, then asks herself.)

      "Was it cold?" Very.
The two of us climbed in that feather bed.
That was a moment I had faced with dread,
Oh, not because of sex, that was a treat,
When we could get it. I refer to heat,
Or lack of. I was sure that death
Would take us both. Why, you could see your breath,
It was so cold. And, so, we snuggled in,
And in a while, I notice we begin
To warm the space beneath the coverlet,
And in the heated bed, a love duet
Begins. From that night on I never rued
The path I'd chosen. Live in solitude?
Not for a fortune. For a happy life,
'Tis better far, my dear, to be a wife.

*From **Life Is A Dream**, by Calderon de la Barca*

(This is the first speech in the play. Rosauro's horse has just run away, depositing her, disguised as a man, in Poland. She has come here to find the lover who deserted her, to regain her honor.)

ROSAURO.

You misbegotten horse! You think yourself
A fiery steed—you try to race the wind,
And dare the birds to catch you! Crazy beast,
Where have you bolted off to, leaving me
Alone on these bare rocks? Well, I can't search
For you. I'll have to leave you here—you hear?
And if the wild beasts eat you, don't blame me!
You have it coming. Where's the path? Nowhere.
My only path's the one that Destiny
Lays out before me. This forbidding rock
Scowls at the sun, and I must grope my way
With tear-wash'd eyes half blind with their despair.
So this is Poland. An unfriendly land!
You greet me with misfortune—what a welcome!
But when I feel the load of grief I've dragged
Behind me as I've traveled, it's no matter.
I've come this far, I will not weaken now!
Unhappy people never get a break.

*From **Andromache** (Ann Dramakey), by Euripides*

Adapted by Freyda Thomas

(**NOTE;** *This is a comic version of the tragedy, set in Texas, with Ann Dramakey a drawling Southerner. The full play is currently being adapted as a comedy. There is also a straight, tragic adaptation of the same monologue available in this book. At the opening of the play, Ann Dramakey enters, sits down at the foot of a statue and lights a cigarette.)*

ANN DRAMAKEY.

Oh, why did I leave home? It was so purty,
Not like this lousy place, all mean and dirty,
But girls get married, don't they? So I went
From east to west,[1] all young and innocent,
A bride with one huge dowry, that was me,
The wife of Hector, Miss Ann Dramakey.
They all knew who I was, back in those days.
I'd say I had it all, to coin a phrase,
Until that stupid fight and that damn horse
With all the men inside. Some fightin' force
They were! That was a day I won't forget.
My kid got thrown right off a parapet,
My hubby, Hector, murdered by Achilles,
Just thinkin' bout it all gives me the willies!
As if that ain't enough, I'm dragged out here
To be a love slave, yep, a souvenir
Of battle. How 'bout that? It makes me cuss
When I remember Neoptolemus,
The son of that dumb jerk who killed my man.
Oh well, us gals just do the best we can,
So I shut up, what is the use complainin'?
Complainin' isn't ever entertainin'.
I made the best of things. I had a kid,
And anything that Neo asked, I did.
I figured one day when my kid had grown,
He'd find some way to get his mama blown
From here. But, damn you, Fate, you come along

1 *Athens, Georgia to Troy, Texas*

And write a whole new chorus to the song.
Neo gets married to some jealous cat
Who'd like to kill me, whaddya think of that!?
Hermione, the dense, the barren wife
Is makin' one big mis'ry of my life.
This chick is nuts! She thinks I'm puttin' spells
On her to keep her childless. Well, hell's bells!
I didn't ask to be her husband's whore!
In point of fact, this whore thinks he's a bore.
But one man's poison… Anyway, her dad
Has just arrived in town, and is he bad!
He wants me dead, this mister Menelouse,
So that's why I have come here to your house
For—what's the word they use? Uh—sanctuary.
You wanna know how worried I am? Very.
I've sent the kid, Molasses, out of town,
'Cause if I don't they'll try to bring him down,
The two of them. And where is Neo? Gone
To Delphi, leaving me to carry on
Without a friend to help me see this through.
Well, don't just stand there, tell me what to do!

From **Andromache** *(Ann Dramakey) by Euripides*

Adapted by Freyda Thomas

(**NOTE**: *This is a comedic version of the tragedy, set in modern day Texas. Hermione is a Texas shrew, pissed off at Ann Dramakey because she is the preferred bed partner of her husband, Neoptolemus (Neo for short). In this scene, Ann is seeking shelter at the statue of Thetis, a sanctuary for people who may be in danger, when Hermione arrives to chew her out.*)

HERMIONE.

Look at this crown. It's gold. It's on my head.
Check out the dress. What does it say? Well-bred!
And all that gorgeous stuff back at the palace?
It's mine. And if you think I'm full of malice,
I am. I have it all, and you have zip,
Which means you do not give me any lip.
You listen. I know what you're after, bitch,
You're puttin' spells on me, just like a witch,
To take my place and make my husband hate me.
I want a baby! God, you irritate me,
You eastern types. Well, let me tell you what:
You won't get help from anybody, slut.
There ain't no altar, statue, God or man
To save you. I will end what I began
And you will learn respect from me, I swear,
You'll kneel and bow, assume a humble air,
Scrub floors, do windows, clean like any maid,
Wash all my laundry, bring me lemonade
Whenever I command you. Hector's[1] gone.
So is your kid–gone to oblivion![2]
And you, I might point out, sleep with the man
Whose father did this to you. There's a plan,
To put some incest in your life for spice,
And sleep with him who killed your husband—nice!
Except, of course, in these parts, where we frown
Upon such seedy morals. In this town
A man has only one wife, never two
And that is definitely me, not you!

1 *Andromache's husband*
2 *Andromache's son, thrown from a parapet to his death*

From **The Misanthrope**

Adapted by Freyda Thomas

*(This homely and prudish young woman who "claims"
to be a friend of Celimène, the lovely and charming, tells
her what "they" are saying about her.)*

ARSINOE.

Dear Celimène, I've come here with a mission,
A noble purpose, born not of ambition
But true concern for one I dare call friend.
I beg you, hear my words and comprehend
The serious intent with which I bring
This news. My dear, I am not lecturing,
But I must speak to you of reputation.
Yours. Last night, in heated conversation
With people known for truth and pious thought,
Your name came up. Do you agree I ought
To tell you how society sees you?
Well, it was not a flattering review,
I fear. They brought up all those hordes of men
Who come to… visit you time and again.
The cheap flirtations you engage upon
With them—they just went on, and on, and on,
And on. They spoke of things so scandalous,
And on this topic made such a big fuss,
Your reputation was called to account,
And reputation is, well, paramount
In good society, I'm sure you know.
Your own is not in very fine tableau
Right now. Don't worry, dear, I took your part.
And spoke with great conviction from the heart.
"High spirited," I said. "She's not aware
That her behavior is in disrepair."
I made excuses, said your heart was good,
That mostly you behave the way you should.
Defended your occas'nal lapse of moral
Rectitude, but they were bent on quarrel
With me. Gossip spreads. One incident
Can lead to scandal. We cannot prevent

The tongues from wagging, vicious lies from spreading
And dragging you—you see where this is heading?
I had to tell you, friend to friend, the news,
So that in future moments, you may choose
A wiser and more prudent path, my dear.
I hope you know that I have been sincere
In telling you this news. My only aim
Is saving you from deep despair and shame.

From **The Misanthrope**, *by Molière*

Adapted by Freyda Thomas

(In The Misanthrope, a beautiful, accomplished, shallow young woman tells off her friend Arsinoé, who has just criticized her for her behavior. For reference, see Arsinoe's monologue.)

CELIMENE.

Arsinoé! My friend! I am beholden
To you. Let me say, your words are golden.
Take badly kind and sage advice? No way!
I am too grateful. But if I may say,
That is, if I might, well, return the favor,
And tell you a few thoughts of such like flavor,
Concerning your own reputation, dear.
You've shown such loyalty, it would appear,
By telling me what has been said of me,
That I would be unkind, I'm sure you see,
If I did not reveal what I just heard
Two days ago. Shall I say what occurred?
A conversation on the topic: virtue.
What does it mean? Now I don't want to hurt you,
But your name did come up. Your piety,
They said, was in excess. Your prudery?
Too ostentatious. And your glum behavior,
They all agreed, would even bore our Savior!
Those everlasting moral sermons you
Seem so hell-bent on giving—well, you do
Go on. And on. They said. "She's the czarina
Of morals and appropriate demeanor."
She loves to stomp on everybody's thought!
"Physician, heal thyself," is what we ought
To say to her," they said. And I know you
Are far too sensible not to construe
This information as good, sound advice,
And in the future, dear, perhaps think twice
Before you criticize another's actions.
Let's leave to God society's distractions,

For Heaven is a better judge than you
Of all the right and moral things to do.
Of course, in telling you, I just intend
To show my true concern for a good friend.

From **The Misanthrope,** *by Molière*

Adapted by Freyda Thomas

(Celimene has finally had it up to here with Alceste's jealous moralizing and confronts him in no uncertain terms.)

CELIMENE.

I'm sick of this! You're one long jealous fit!
You don't deserve to be loved—not one bit!
Why did I ever want to be attached
To such a man? We are too far mismatched
To make a go of this. You don't trust me.
I tell you with complete sincerity
That I am yours, and bing! The slightest rumor
Throws you into such a morbid humor
That all I want to do is run away.
Why should I want a man who thinks I play
With his affections? Why should I spend time
With someone who thinks smiling is a crime!?
Who will not take my word, who won't believe
That I'm sincere? Why don't you go? Just leave!
And when you understand a woman's heart,
Come back. Until that day we stay apart.
I just can't go through this again—these scenes!
They're so exhausting—boring! If that means
That I must seek out someone else's arms
Then so be it. You're running low on charms,
My dear. This woman wants a little fun,
And your behavior says you're not the one
To have it with. I'll have a wild, insane
Affair, then you'll have reason to complain!

From **Tartuffe: Born Again,** *by Molière*

Adapted by Freyda Thomas

*(Orgon's beautiful wife recognizes that her husband will
not believe anything bad of Tartuffe, so she invents a
plan to expose the hypocrite to Orgon. She explains the
strategy to him in this monologue.)*

ELMIRE.

All right. You're going to see with your own eyes
Tartuffe's deception, trickeries and lies.
I'll make you see and hear without a doubt,
Exactly what Tartuffe is all about.
It's clear at least that I have got to try,
But you, my dear, have got to stay nearby.
You'll hide right under there.

(She points to a table with a cloth cover.)

Before we start,
Remember, I'm not speaking from my heart.
I'll be... playacting, only to reveal
That your beloved preacher is a heel.
I'll flatter him, pretend that I admire
His mind and his physique, that I desire
The liaison that he proposed, you see?
Remember, this is feigned sincerity,
Designed to coax that hypocrite to drop
His mask and show his true self. I won't stop
Until you choose to end this scene. Don't wait
Too long. It's up to you to calculate
How far to let him go with me. His lust
Is, at the least, unbridled, so you must
Come out the moment you have heard enough.
I warn you. Things might get a little rough
Out here. I don't mind telling you I'm very
Nervous. Wait no more than necessary.

*From **Tartuffe: Born Again,** by Molière*

Adapted by Freyda Thomas

(Orgon's obedient Southern belle daughter must choose between being banished from her father's house or marrying Tartuffe.)

MARYANN.
I just can't marry him! Oh, Daddy, please!
I can't! I'm begging you on bended knees!
I'm so unhappy, can't I move your heart
To reconsider? I am torn apart.
Don't make me choose between you and my love.
I've always tried to place your wants above
All others, but my heart has found a voice,
And, sadly, it has made another choice.
I'm happy for you, Daddy, in your flight
With your Tartuffe to Heaven's holy light,
I heartily approve—build him a shrine,
Give him your love, your money-give him mine!
But if you won't consent to let me dwell
In Paradise with Val, do not compel
This marriage that would bring me misery
My whole life long. Please, don't do this to me!
I'd sooner leave you and have you disown
Me—cast me out to spend my life alone.

*From **Tartuffe: Born Again,** by Molière*

Adapted by Freyda Thomas

(Moliere's most famous and sassiest maid–a floor manager of an evangelical TV station in this version–tells Cleante what's been going on while he was away, and how Tartuffe—a deposed televangelist– has taken over the family.)

DORINE.

You see? She[1] gets more crazy every day,
And meanwhile, this Tartuffe won't go away.
The situation's very serious—
You won't believe the way they make a fuss!
And she's a saint compared to what Orgon
Is doing. How they love to carry on!
And he was once a government official,
A figure of respect in the judicial
Circuit- Why, he earned a reputation
For wisdom, and the country's admiration.
Now he cries "Brother!" hugs him like a child,
Regales Tartuffe with gorgeous gifts, goes wild
With worry if the snake so much as sneezes.
Swears that he'll stay by him until hell freezes,
Ignores his fam'ly—daughter, son and wife,
In staunch pursuit of "the religious life."

(Indicates the TV studio they are standing in.)

Look at this studio! Bought for him! The cost!
You do not want to know how much was lost.
Meanwhile, the subject of our problem here
Is in, a word or two, a profiteer!
It's sad to watch. Tartuffe's become his hero.
And if you're asking me, the man's a zero,
Except for his ability to deceive.
He plays Orgon for all he's worth, believe
You me. Gets money out of him like that.
He knows just where his bread is buttered at.
Sound bad? He's master of our lives, in fact.

1 Orgon's mother

He reprimands the slightest, harmless act,
Tells all of us our lifestyle is a crime,
He talks and talks and....he talks all the time.
It's just a shame, a real disgrace to see
That man take over this whole family,
And tell us what we can and cannot do.
Lightheartedness and laughter are taboo,
We're totally forbidden to express
A simple thought. In short, things are a mess!

From **The Learnéd Ladies,** *by Molière*

Adapted by Freyda Thomas

(The elder sister of Henriette expounds on the joys of knowledge over marriage.)

ARMANDE.

Good Lord, your mind's in such a low estate
That you are telling me you choose this fate?
In household's prison, asking to be locked
With spouse and screaming babies? Well, I'm shocked.
My dear, you must give up this foolish goal.
Through knowledge you will elevate your soul
And leave the burdens of domestic life
To other women, who enjoy the strife.
When one gets married, intellectual
Pursuits are simply ineffectual.
How can one think when all one's time is spent
In housework and domestic management?
Please, set your mind at high consideration
And think a bit of mother's liberation.
The eyes of learnéd men are fast upon her,
And not with lust, but deference and honor.
I'd sing your praise as learnéd far and wide,
Before I'd stoop to sing, "Here Comes the Bride."
Oh, Henriette, it's truly rapturous
To study differential calculus!
It's hard at first, but what a satisfaction
The first time you make sense of such abstraction!
Read Carl Sagan on astronomy,
Boyle's elements and Greek philosophy,
Jacques Derrida on deconstruction—thrilling!
Such studies are rewarding and fulfilling.
This wealth of knowledge is what should inspire you,
And not some man, who thinks he might desire you,
And make you slave to laws devised by men.
Philosophy must be your husband then.
Its very nature serves to elevate
Our souls to heights at which we may create

Environs where our lust can have no sway,
Where carnal passions can be kept at bay.
Thus, thoughts of pleasure have no ill effects
And one can turn one's back on S-E-X.

From **The Learned Ladies,** *by Molière*

Adapted by Freyda Thomas

(The younger sister of Armande explains to her "liberated" sister that she just wants to get married.)

HENRIETTE.

Sweet sister, from our Lord we've been ordained
With different functions. What is to be gained
From being something I'm not meant to be?
If you want to espouse philosophy,
The heights of worthy, learnéd speculation,
Go for it! I prefer domestication.
Let's not disturb what Heaven has arranged.
I do not want my instincts to be changed.
I'm happy for you in your worldly flight
To great philosophy's stupendous height,
But flying to me is one of those things
For which God would endow us all with wings
If we were meant to fly. So leave me here,
In earthly bliss and pure domestic cheer,
To follow mother in her lesser role,
But one which helps to elevate her soul.
If mother's who you wish to imitate
Then let both aspects serve us to create
The model. And, my sister, think on this:
We'd not be here if not for wedded bliss.
The basest parts of marriage, as you say,
Are what gave all of us the light of day,
And I, for one, applaud the time she chose a
Moment to forget Kant and Spinoza.
Accept with grace this marriage that I want,
And maybe I'll produce a new savant!

From **The Learned Ladies,** *by Molière*

Adapted by Freyda Thomas

(The older sister and liberated woman discovers that the green-eyed monster has bitten her. Though she professes to prefer learning to romance, her pride is wounded and she has just finished telling her equally liberated mother that her younger sister is planning to marry Clitandre, who wanted to marry her not long ago. She is discovered by him spilling the beans and must defend her position.)

ARMANDE.

And so, you found me out. I don't deny it.
I'm angry, sir, and I can justify it
Easily. It's but too well-deserved.
A heart that has been wooed becomes unnerved
When fickleness makes it renounce the one
Who had desired it. To be undone
By such a change of heart is just obscene,
And he who caused it all is small and mean.
You say I was opposed to your desires?
It was, in fact, to purge them of the fires
Of lewd and vulgar lust which they contained,
In order to perceive a love unstained
And pure. One must extract true love from lust
And let it brightly shine. But you! You must
Declare yourself with passion, and enmesh
Your love with base expressions of the flesh.
You're so obsessed with love material!
True love needs only an ethereal
Environment to taste its sweetest charms.
But you can't love without your bearing arms
And bringing forms of physicality
Into the fore…play. Such impurity
Of soul has no place where true love exists.
It burns with flames to clear away the mists
Of physical desires that make it shoddy.
One then expresses love without one's body.

From **The Learned Ladies**, *by Molière*

Adapted by Freyda Thomas

*(The classic Molière maid, simple with a world of common
sense, tells her mistress, Philamente, exactly what she
thinks of Trissotin, the pseudo-intellectual trickster she's
taken in. Sound a little like Tartuffe? Molière was not
above stealing from himself, as well as anyone else who
had a good plot, including and especially Plautus.)*

MARTINE.

Speak plainly? Good, Well, plain means honest too,
So, plainly, I will speak the truth to you.
Before a certain party came to stay
This was a happy home in every way.
Oh sure, you spouted lots of fancy phrases,
And made me fill the vahses, not the vayses,
Corrected what I said at every turn,
But that's all right with me. I like to learn
A thing or two, once in a while, for fun.
But now the situation's overdone,
And why? Because a certain pompous ass
Sees fit to criticize the underclass!
Berates the way we talk to make himself
Climb higher on his high and mighty shelf.
To whooom do I refer? To whooom indeed!
A man whose name's a cinnamon for greed!
You took him in, and here's the awful sin,
You are the one who's being taken in.

*From **Splitting Heirs**, by Freyda Thomas (inspired by Le Legataire Universel, by Jean-François Regnard)*

(**NOTE:** *This monologue can be performed by male or female. Crispin is the classic, crafty servant who explains her philosophy of life and work.*)

CRISPIN.
A servant's life is not an easy one.
But then again, whose life is naught but fun?
Who does not sometime, somewhere in one's life
Experience a small degree of strife?
And though I may have more than others felt
The gnaw of hunger tight'ning at my belt,
Or once and frequently been forced to greet
The frosty nip of winter at my feet,
The chilblains in my joints from chopping wood,
In general, my life's been rather good!
A servant's life may have its ups and downs,
But truly, do the heads that wear the crowns
Lie easier than ours? I say nay, nay.
A servant's life may not be distingué,
And emptying of chamber pots may not
Be your idea of a grand gavotte,
Or climbing stairs or weeding gardens or
The washing and a hundred errands more,
But I'm not wont to dwell in dark despair,
For in here is much better than out there,
And wishing one were elsewhere than where one
Has found oneself to be is best not done.
So, though the concept seems a bit demented
And seeped in optimism, I'm contented!
Lament? Complain? Bemoan? Why, what's the good?
I'd not trade places with them if I could.
You think they're any happier than we?
Just watch how things progress and you will see.

*From **Scapin,** by Molière*

Adapted by Freyda Thomas

(Zerbinette, a lovely gypsy girl, reveals the plot Scapin has come up with to dupe her sweetheart's father and get money out of him. Of course, she is talking to her sweetheart's father without knowing it. This monologue works well if you choose a man in the audience, class, or behind the table and pretend he's the father.)

ZERBINETTE.
You want to hear the story? Well, why not?
By evening someone will have told the plot.
It starts far from here, in some hinterland.
A child is born into a gypsy band—
C'est moi. We travel, they teach me my trade,
I sing, tell fortunes, sometimes I am paid
A coin or two. The crowds think I'm a treat!
I smile, I bow, my manners are discreet,
And then one day we stumble on this place,
And a young man takes one look at my face
And ping! He's smitten. He's in love with me.
And if he is I must be too, you see.
But, he discovers I'm not easily had.
Of course, the truth is I was very glad,
But dared not show it. He went to my clan.
"You want to steal her from our caravan!?
Oh, what a vile suggestion, sir. No thanks,
Unless of course you pay 500 francs."
Now, this young man was slightly upper class,
But had no funds. His father is an ass—
A miser to the nth degree, but rich,
So here's what happened—this is such a stitch!—
The young man has a servant called Scapin,
Who came up with a very clever plan
To get the cash from that old miser man
And pay those greedy people from my clan.
He told that skinflint—ha! Wait till you hear!—
There were three Turkish pirates near the pier
Where they were walking. There was conversation,

Soon followed by a luncheon invitation
Aboard their ship, the servant said. So he
Just climbed aboard, Scapin, the pirates three,
And he. The pirates locked him down below,
And said that this Scapin should forthwith go
And tell the father, if he did not pay
To have his son released that very day,
Then he would realize his darkest fears,
And sonny would be carted to Algiers—
Sold as a slave! Meanwhile the old curmudgeon,
Though he struggles, isn't yet begrudgin'
The sum of money asked. Five hundred francs!
Oh, isn't this the funniest of pranks?
The servant made the whole thing up! I swear,
To see the old man's face—wish I'd been there!

    (dropping her voice)

"What shall I do!? My child—but oh, my money!"
Ha-ha! How come you don't think this is funny?

From **School for Trophy Wives**, *by Molière*

Adapted by Freyda Thomas

*(A completely naïve young Agnes explains to her much
older guardian, who plans to marry her himself, how she
came to meet a young man.)*

AGNES.

It's such a story, one you'd never think
Would happen to a girl from Humperdink,
And when you hear it, you'll know I did right.
Why, thinkin' of it gives me such a fright!
Well, here's what happened. On the balcony,
Just sittin' in the sunshine, there was me,
Enjoyin' all of nature's wonders rare,
The trees, the bees, the birds, the mornin' air,
It was a lovely day. I looked around,
And then, by chance, my eyes dropped to the ground,
And there was this young man. He smiled and waved,
And so I waved. Well, it would be depraved
Of me if I decided to ignore
A man with such good manners. So, therefore,
I waved. He waved again, and smiled to boot.
Well, what else could I do? I followed suit
And smiled right back at him. And waved again.
He smiled and waved, I waved and smiled....and then...
I think he smiled once more and went away.
And then, let's see, I think it was...next day,
I went out on the balcony to greet
The morning, like before...the air was sweet,
That next day, with the birds, the bees, the air,
I look down, and my goodness, standing there,
Where he had stood the day before, I see
An old, old woman. She looks up at me,
Says, "Bless you, senorita." "Bless you too,"
I say. She says, "El Dio gave you beauty,
So I must do for him my sacred duty
And tell you that you've wounded someone." "Oh!"
I say. But how this happened I don't know.
Perhaps I dropped a pot on someone's head

And split it open. Someone might be dead!
"What did I do!?" "Sus ojos[1]…" "What?" "Your eyes,"
She said, "Are weapons to effect the sad demise
Of any man who sees them." "Is that true?"
I asked. She nods. "Oh, dear, what should I do!?"
"You must agree to see the man whose heart
From one look in your eyes is torn apart,
For nothing but a kindly look from you
Can save him from the torment he's been through."
"That's all I have to do?" "That's all," says she.
"Well, shoot, that's nothin', send him right to me."
Why, I'd be crueler than the cruelest cad
If I did not agree. "Si, I am glad,"
She says. "He'll come to you tomorrow.
One look from you will banish all his sorrow,"
And so it was! He came and looked and ping!
He cheered right up! It made me want to sing.

   (*She sings, badly, then looks at* **Arnolphe**.)

You look a little funny. Was I wrong
To help him? Oh, you didn't like the song!
Well, you know how I am. I just can't bear
To think of anybody suffering. There,
You've got to smile for me, or else I'll cry,
If I thought I had hurt you, I would die!

1 OH-hos

*From **The Triumph of Love**, by Marivaux*

Adapted by Freyda Thomas

*(At the very beginning of this play, the young servant
Hermidas has just arrived at the residence of Hemocrate,
a popular philosopher. She has come with her lady,
Phocion , at her insistence, and both are dressed in drag.
Hermidas is clueless to why they are there, why they are
dressed like men, and why her Mistress won't tell her.)*

HERMIDAS.

Voilá, we've arrived. We are, in a word, planted in the gardens of Hemocrate, the renowned philosopher. We don't
know a soul here, we'll no doubt be arrested for trespass-
ing. You've left your home, your city, you've given me not
one clue as to why we're doing this, but I'm your servant,
I have to follow you to your country house, which I do,
with still no explanation. You make me take-up painting,
and loyal servant that I am, I do, and I'm pretty good at it,
as it turns out, especially with two portraits you give me to
copy in miniature, which is probably against the law, now
that I think of it. The moment I finish my handiwork, you
suddenly announce that you are indisposed—you will see
no one. But does it stop there? Of course not. You dress
yourself and me in men's clothes and we hightail it out of
town in your coach and for what? You change our names,
I am now to be called Hermidas and you Phocion—you
could at least have let me pick out my own name!—and
we gallop apace from our very comfortable residence in
the city for a good 15 minutes, stop the coach, ditch the
coach, and end up here in the gardens of a philosopher
who appeals to you as much as dental work does. You may
conclude from this diatribe that I might have a few ques-
tions knocking around in my head, such as, what the hell
are we doing here!?

*From **Splitting Heirs**, by Freyda Thomas (inspired by Le Legataire Universel by Regnard)*

(The prettiest, dumbest ingenue ever, possibly with a lisp, grabs the epilogue at the end of the play and demands her 15 minutes of fame. Throughout the play she has never had more than 3 words in a row to say.)

ISABELLE.

Now just a minute! All who did this play
Have had a pretty peck of words to say,
Except for me. Not even one small speech!
So please forgive me for this awkward breach
Of manners, but I mean to have my say,
And speak the final passage of this play.

(She reads from the paper.)

Good ladies, gentlemen, to well present
The mask of comedy was our intent.
And if, perchance, a feeling pierced your soul,
Inspired by this modest….

(She struggles to read the word.)

barcarole,
Then we have labored well, for what's a play?
A flow'ring of our thought, a sweet bouquet
Of sights and sighs and sounds, all joys and woes
Enwoven in mercurial tableaux.
A lucent crystal mirror to this plane.
But in this purpose here to entertain
We are no more than silence gone unheard
Without the listening ear to hear the word
And cheer the effort here within this hall,

(She acknowledges audience.)

And so to you—great players one and all!

*From **The Imaginary Cuckold,** by Molière*

Adapted by Freyda Thomas

*(Martine has been leaning out the window, watching her
husband fondle the breast of a fainted woman—when in
fact he's checking to see if she's alive. Her husband and
the fainted girl exit before Martine gets downstairs.)*

MARTINE

Hey, hey! What's going on down there!? Aha!
My husband with a girl and it's not moi!
Just wait until I catch you, here I come!

(She starts down a winding staircase.)

You cool conniving cheat, you think I'm dumb
Or something? I know your game—keep me busy,
While you fool around with—hey, where is he?
How did he disappear so quickly? What
Is going on!!?? He was right on this spot,
His hand on that girl's –hold on, where is she!?
Oh, maybe I was dreaming, that could be.
Oh no, I wasn't! Now I know why he
For weeks has not so much as looked at me!
I get it now, those cold, unfeeling stares
While I am starved for—ha, a lot he cares.
He's saving up to feast on some young thing,
And what do I get? Just a wedding ring!
These men—how do they get away with this!!??
Where has his conscience gone? Where's wedded bliss?
Oh, when we started out, he was on fire—
It was exhausting, quenching his desire,
But fun. And very, very satisfying.
And then one day, he's bored. But I keep trying
To entice, seduce, get him to yield,
But no, he wants to plow another field.
I've had it! Now I'm ready for a fight!
Come on, you women of the world, unite!

MATURE WOMEN'S COMEDIC MONOLOGUES

From **The Gamester**, *by Freyda Thomas (inspired by Le Joueur by Regnard)*

(Mme. Securité is a woman of a certain age who gives young men money in exchange for favors. She has just had a session with one, who lies, out cold, upstage of her while she rearranges her hair and make-up. She speaks directly to the audience. **NOTE:** *When performing in class, it's effective to ask a fellow classmate to play the sleeping young man.)*

MME. SECURITE.
A maid, 'twixt twelve and twenty ought to be
The soul of innocence and purity.
Naive, exuberant, a budding rose,
So pliant in the hands of eager beaux.
She whispers, "Teach me how to do my duty."
Of course it is essential she have beauty.
The next 10 years, the lady must be sure
To cultivate a slightly ripe allure.
She knows the way, but hasn't learned it all,
In case some afternoon you chance to call
While hubby's safely sheltered at his club,
She'll learn a few new things–ay, there's the rub!
From thirty till she's forty she must be
Endowed with wit and personality.
She shines in the salon, she sparkles plenty,
Convinces you that she's but one and twenty.
She laughs and quips, a true comedienne,
She's talked about by women and by men,
Yet both seek out her charming company,
A fascinating sorceress is she.

Yet when she is alone, and forty plus,
And all those people cease to make a fuss,
She looks into the glass, and tiny fears
Creep up like lines that steal away her years.
Sweet youth beyond her grasp. She sighs and cries,
Not quite content that age will make her wise,
Yet wise she must become, what can she do?
One look into the glass says she is through,
Her precious beauty gone in one bright flash.

> *(She stands, tosses a bag of coins on the sleeping man and starts to exit.)*

Oh, if she lives past fifty? She needs cash.

From **Tartuffe: Born Again,** *by Molière*

Adapted by Freyda Thomas

(Orgon's mother, a very old southern lady, is fed up with her family's deprecation of her beloved Tartuffe. She opens the play with this monologue, warning of dire consequences if they do not take her pet preacher to their bosom.)

MRS. PERNELL.

Stop all this dilly-dallying–Come on!
From this place I am going, going, gone!
And why? Because I cannot bear to see
The inconsideration shown to me.
Each time we have a meetin' I think, "Good."
This time you'll all behave the way you should,
But no! Nobody heeds my good advice!
I'm given no respect! Now, is that nice?
No! Everybody has to have his say.
You wonder why I want to get away?
It's Babylon, the way you babble on.
Good God, the torments I have undergone,
Because you will not listen to Tartuffe,
That paragon of men, the living proof
That piety makes saints of men. How true—
You hold your tongue, he cares for all of you!
This man my son has fostered is a gift,
A gift from God sent to us to uplift
Our souls from all the muck in which we dwell,
The muck that sends the lot of us to hell!
This blesséd man will offer no reproof
That isn't based on sin, this man, Tartuffe.
Let him pursue his path and he'll restore a
House that acts like Sodom and Gomorrah!
Now listen up, you're in this corporation
My son has founded—I want dedication!
I'm given him my power of attorney
To take us on our spiritual journey
With this...

(Waving her arm around the TV studio.)

... to lead us all to Heaven's Gate,
And all you want to do is deprecate
Tartuffe, who has the power to take us there.
So, you'll support this man, or else I swear
I'll cut you off without a single dime!
I've argued over this for the last time.

From **The Learned Ladies,** *by Molière*

Adapted by Freyda Thomas

(The "liberated" head of the family sits at her desk, composing a liberating speech. **NOTE:** *This is completely original, not in the original text of Molière's penultimate play.)*

PHILAMENTE.
"Dear members of the fellowship of mind…"
Oh no, not fellowship, that's too behind
The times, a biased word if e'er I heard one.
Let's see now, sisterhood! That's the preferred one.
"Dear members of the sisterhood of mind:
A noble purpose calls us, of the kind
Which changes ever more man's destiny."
Whoops! Woman's destiny. Now let me see.
"Henceforward, women of the world be free!"
Well, that's a good beginning. On the mark.
Inspire, and then hit them with the spark
Of rousing rhetoric. Good. To continue…
"I charge you, fellow sisters, find within you—"
Oh! Fellow sisters! There it is again!
Now stop that, you're a naughty little pen.
Change that to…sister citizens. That's sweet.
"All sister citizens, rise up to meet
The challenge of our times! With heads held high
We'll march into the future with the cry,
No more will we be second class! No more!
Our liberty is knocking at the door,
And we must cry, 'Come in!' We're ready now,
For everything that freedom will allow,
All past injustices we shall address—"
A dress? I'll wear the yellow one—yes, yes!

From the Reviews of
50 FABULOUS CLASSICAL
MONOLOGUES FOR WOMEN...

"This collection will be a delight and an
invaluable resource for actors everywhere."
- Carey Perloff, Artistic Director, American Conservatory Theatre

"Every actor must have this invaluable
collection of fresh, eminently actable monologues."
- Ron Lagomarsino, Broadway, Regional and TV director

"A treasure trove of wonderful new classical material
for auditions, classes and practice of our craft."
- Mark Zimmerman, President, Actors' Equity Association

"Actors, buy this book! Whether you're searching for something
serious or comic, Thomas and Silverman bring
extraordinary new life to these classic monologues."
- Jack W. Batman, Producer/Executive Producer,
White Plains Performing Arts Center

"A surprising selection, sure to make an actor's audition a standout."
- B.J. Jones, Artistic Director, Northlight Theatre

CPSIA information can be obtained at www.ICGtesting.com
Printed in the USA
BVOW11s1557200815

414037BV00007B/61/P

9 780573 662737